Let's Celebrate American Holidays

Veterans Day

Katie Gillespie

LET'S READ
AV2 BY WEIGL
ADDED VALUE • AUDIO VISUAL

LET'S READ
AV²
BY WEIGL™
ADDED VALUE • AUDIO VISUAL

Go to **www.av2books.com,**
and enter this book's
unique code.

BOOK CODE

S 3 9 4 5 8 4

AV² by Weigl brings you media
enhanced books that support
active learning.

AV² provides enriched content that supplements and complements this book. Weigl's AV² books strive to create inspired learning and engage young minds in a total learning experience.

Your AV² Media Enhanced books come alive with...

Audio
Listen to sections of
the book read aloud.

Video
Watch informative
video clips.

Embedded Weblinks
Gain additional information
for research.

Try This!
Complete activities and
hands-on experiments.

Key Words
Study vocabulary, and
complete a matching
word activity.

Quizzes
Test your knowledge.

Slide Show
View images and
captions, and prepare
a presentation.

... and much, much more!

Published by AV² by Weigl
350 5th Avenue, 59th Floor New York, NY 10118
Website: www.av2books.com

Library of Congress Control Number: 2015934752

ISBN 978-1-4896-3637-9 (hardcover)
ISBN 978-1-4896-3638-6 (softcover)
ISBN 978-1-4896-3639-3 (single user eBook)
ISBN 978-1-4896-3640-9 (multi-user eBook)

Printed in the United States of America in Brainerd, Minnesota
1 2 3 4 5 6 7 8 9 0 19 18 17 16 15

072015
070715

Editor: Katie Gillespie   Design and Layout: Ana María Vidal

Let's Celebrate American Holidays

Veterans Day

CONTENTS

Veterans Day is celebrated on November 11th every year. It is a day to give thanks to everyone who has served in the United States military.

Veterans Day was first called Armistice Day because of an important peace agreement.

6

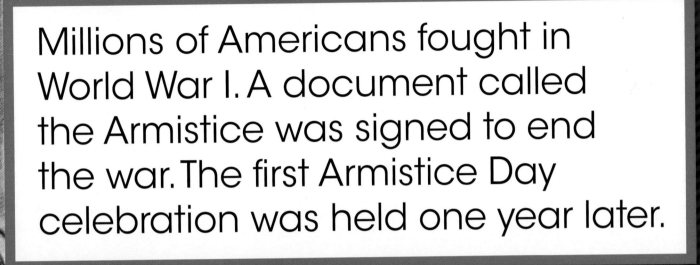

Millions of Americans fought in World War I. A document called the Armistice was signed to end the war. The first Armistice Day celebration was held one year later.

Armistice Day came to be known as Veterans Day in 1954.

Almost every country in the world took part in World War I. It lasted from 1914 to 1918.

The United States joined the war in 1917.

9

The first Veterans Day parade took place in Birmingham, Alabama. It recognized the service of all American veterans.

Veterans Day parades are now held across America.

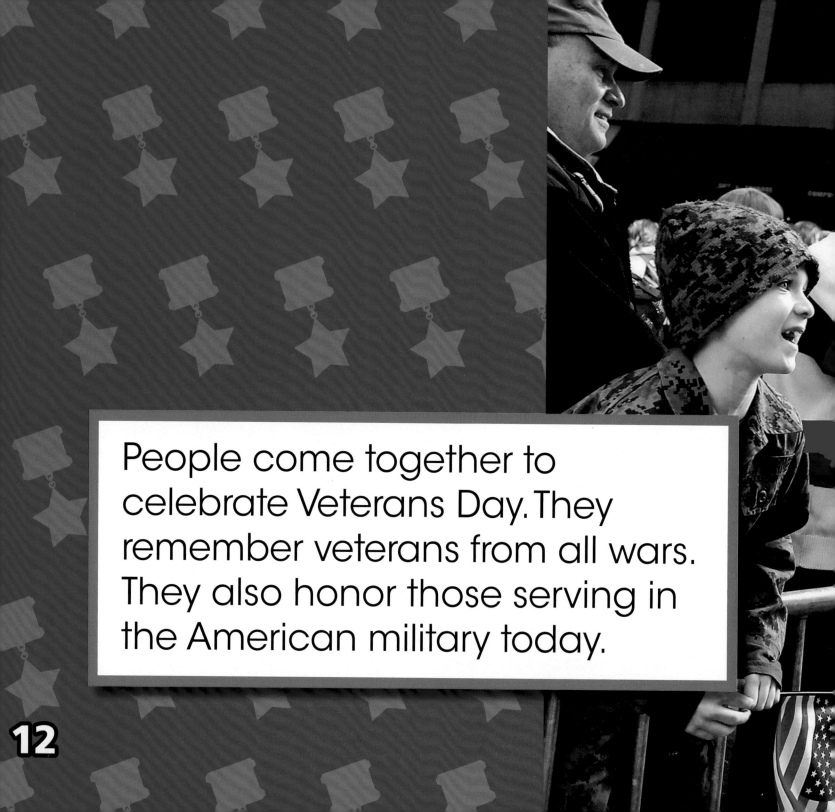

People come together to celebrate Veterans Day. They remember veterans from all wars. They also honor those serving in the American military today.

13

Special events are held across the country. One of the most important ceremonies takes place at the Tomb of the Unknowns in Arlington, Virginia.

Wreaths are placed in memory of those who lost their lives in battle.

The poppy was made an official memorial flower in 1922. People wear poppies on Veterans Day as a sign of respect.

"WEAR IT PROUDLY"

17

National Veterans Awareness Week is held in November. Students learn how veterans helped to protect their freedom.

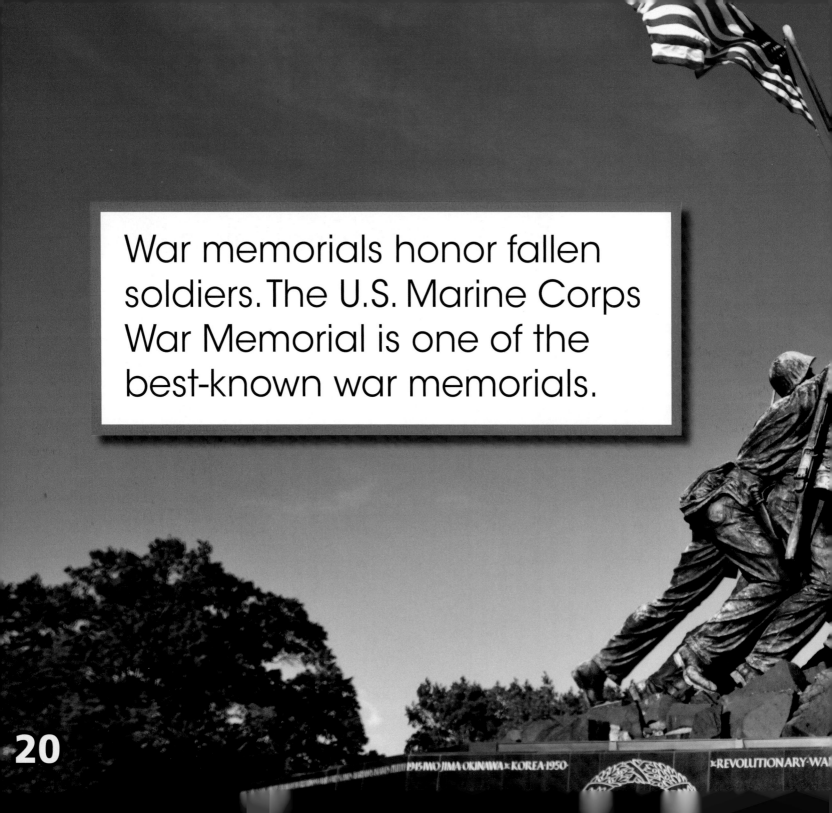

War memorials honor fallen soldiers. The U.S. Marine Corps War Memorial is one of the best-known war memorials.

The memorial's flag flies 24 hours a day, 365 days a year.

783 × FRENCH NAVAL WAR 1798-1801 × TRIPOLI 1801-1805 × WAR OF 1812-1815 × FLORIDA INDIAN WARS 1835-1842

VETERANS DAY FACTS

These pages provide more detail about the interesting facts found in the book. They are intended to be used by adults as a learning support to help young readers round out their knowledge of each holiday featured in the *Let's Celebrate American Holidays* series.

Pages 4–5

Veterans Day is celebrated on November 11th every year. It is a day to remember American war veterans and peacekeepers. Originally called Armistice Day, the first celebrations were held in 1919. They featured public meetings, parades, and a moment of silence. By 1926, Armistice Day had become an official holiday in 27 American states. It became a national holiday in 1938.

Pages 6–7

Millions of Americans fought in World War I. The Armistice marked the end of combat at 11:11 am on November 11, 1918. People celebrated the victory all over the United States by cheering and dancing in the streets. Businesses shut their doors for the day in honor of those who had died. In 1919, President Woodrow Wilson declared November 11th to be Armistice Day. President Dwight D. Eisenhower changed the name of the holiday to Veterans Day in 1954.

Pages 8–9

Almost every country in the world took part in World War I. It was an international conflict that took place between two groups, known as the Central Powers and the Allied Powers. The United States fought on the Allied side, along with 27 other countries. The Central Powers were made up mainly of Germany, Austria-Hungary, and the Ottoman Empire. The war caused more destruction than any other before it. More than 116,000 American soldiers lost their lives.

Pages 10–11

The first Veterans Day parade took place in Birmingham, Alabama. The parade was organized in 1947 by a veteran named Raymond Weeks. He went on to receive a special award called the Presidential Citizens Medal. It was presented in November 1982 by President Reagan. Today, local parades and other festivities have become yearly events that are celebrated across America.

People come together to celebrate Veterans Day. Special events take place across the United States. The Veterans Homecoming in Branson, Missouri, is "America's largest Veterans Day celebration." This week-long tribute features both formal ceremonies and recreational activities, such as hot air balloon rides. Many of the events are free to the public.

Special events are held across the country. People often place flags or flowers upon graves of veterans as an act of remembrance. The Veterans Day National Ceremony is held at the Arlington National Cemetery. It begins with the laying of a wreath on the Tomb of the Unknowns. This memorial honors unknown soldiers who died in World War I, World War II, the Korean War, and the Vietnam War.

The poppy was made an official memorial flower in 1922. After World War I, an American named Moina Michael started to sell poppies made out of paper. She used the money she raised to help support war veterans. People still donate money to buy poppies today. They wear them in honor of military personnel who served or continue to serve their country, both in times of war and peace.

National Veterans Awareness Week is held in November. This resolution was passed by the U.S. Senate in 2001. It focuses on both education and commemoration. National Veterans Awareness Week teaches elementary and secondary school students about the sacrifices and contributions of veterans. It is also a reminder of the importance of providing support services for America's military heroes.

War memorials honor fallen soldiers. The United States Marine Corps Memorial symbolizes America's gratitude toward Marines who have sacrificed their lives for their country. It depicts an iconic flag-raising that took place during World War II on the island of Iwo Jima. The statue is dedicated not only to the men involved in that incident, but to all Marines who have died in defense of the United States since 1775.

KEY WORDS

Research has shown that as much as 65 percent of all written material published in English is made up of 300 words. These 300 words cannot be taught using pictures or learned by sounding them out. They must be recognized by sight. This book contains 51 common sight words to help young readers improve their reading fluency and comprehension. This book also teaches young readers several important content words, such as proper nouns. These words are paired with pictures to aid in learning and improve understanding.

Page	Sight Words First Appearance
4	a, an, because, day, every, first, give, has, important, in, is, it, of, on, the, to, was, who, year
7	Americans, as, be, came, end, known, later, one
8	almost, country, from, part, took, world
11	all, are, now, place
12	also, come, people, they, those, together
14	at, most, takes
15	lives, their
16	made
19	how, learn

Page	Content Words First Appearance
4	Armistice Day, everyone, November, peace agreement, thanks, United States military, Veterans Day
7	Armistice, celebration, document, World War I
8	United States
11	Birmingham, Alabama, parade, service, veterans
14	Arlington, Virginia, ceremonies, events, Tomb of the Unknowns
15	battle, memory, wreaths
16	flower, poppy
19	freedom, National Veterans Awareness Week, students
20	memorials, soldiers, U.S. Marine Corps War Memorial
21	flag

 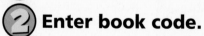